MINI PIÑATAS

Katie Hewat

hinkler

About This Book

This book contains everything you need to know to create some amazing mini piñatas that can be filled with treats or used as ornaments or decorations!

For great results you will need:

- A protective sheet to cover your workspace
- Old newspapers
- Papier-mâché glue (made from flour, water and salt, see page 7)
- Round and oval balloons
- A metal skewer
- Thick and thin paintbrushes
- Coloured paint
- Scissors
- Craft glue
- Cardboard in various colours
- Crepe paper in various colours
- Paper in various colours
- Thick string or twine
- Masking tape
- A graphite or lead pencil
- Pipe cleaners
- Googly eyes
- Tracing paper
- Curling ribbon
- Scalloping scissors
- Ribbon
- A cardboard cup or egg carton cup
- Sequins

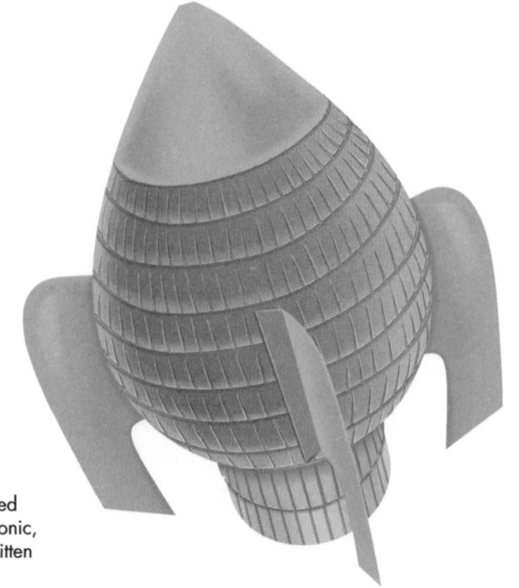

Published by Hinkler Books Pty Ltd
45–55 Fairchild Street
Heatherton Victoria 3202 Australia
www.hinkler.com

Author: Katie Hewat
Internal design: Julie Hally
Cover design: Lizzy Dee Studio
Photography: Ned Meldrum
Illustrations: Brijbasi Art Press Ltd
Prepress: Splitting Image

ISBN: 978 1 4889 3468 1

Printed and bound in China

Contents

All About Piñatas

What Are Piñatas?

Piñatas are bright, hand-crafted models that are filled with different kinds of goodies. Piñatas are traditionally associated with Mexican culture, but have become super popular the world over.

The most iconic piñatas are the traditional Mexican donkeys, but they can be any animal, object or shape that you can imagine – and you'll find lots of cool and original ideas in this book. While the piñatas projects you'll find here are all miniature, you can adjust them to be any size at all by starting with a bigger base and increasing the quantity of other materials to match.

Piñatas are most often found at parties and celebrations, where they are strung from a tree branch so that blindfolded party-goers can take it in turns to whack them with a stick, with the aim of breaking them open and releasing all the goodies inside. Then it's a rush to see who can gather up the most goodies before they're all gone!

You can also make piñatas to keep instead of smashing them – a lot of hard work goes into making them after all! Not only are mini piñatas adorable, but they can also be used as decorative ornaments, party decorations, storage boxes, gifts and much more. You will find fun ideas for what you can do with each mini-piñata project in this book.

What Goes Inside a Mini Piñata?

If you choose to fill your mini piñata, you can put anything you like inside – sweets, toys, glitter or confetti, or even a mixture of them all. Two very important points to keep in mind are:

- Make sure any food items are wrapped, as they will fall to the ground once the piñata breaks open.
- The items that you choose will need to be small enough to fit through the opening in the piñata.

Where Do I Display or Hang My Mini Piñata?

If you are making your mini piñata as an ornament, you can display it anywhere you like, as long as it is indoors – your piñata will not withstand wind or rain. Because it is made from paper, it can also be highly flammable, so be sure to keep it away from potential fire hazards such as candles, lights, heaters and stoves.

If you plan to smash your mini piñata, you will need to find a suitable place to hang it. The best place to hang your piñata is from a tree branch or outdoor rafter. It's best not to hang it inside, as it can be dangerous to have a blindfolded person waving around a whacking stick indoors (even a mini one!), and when the goodies fall out, it can be quite messy.

The projects in this book all suggest a common string length for hanging your mini piñatas, but if your chosen hanging place is higher up, simply extend the length of string that you use. Choose crafting string that is strong enough to support the weight of your mini-piñata.

Getting Started

Constructing Your Mini Piñata

There are two types of piñatas in this book: ones made of papier-mâché and ones made of sturdy card and masking tape.

Papier-mâché Mini Piñatas

You make the papier-mâché mini piñatas in this book from newspaper dipped in glue and wrapped around balloons to form a hard shell. Here are the basic steps to follow:

1. Making papier-mâché can be very messy, so cover your work area with a protective sheet before you begin.
2. Cut old sheets of newspaper into strips roughly 2.5 cm (1 in) wide and 7–10 cm (3–4 in) long.
3. Make your papier-mâché glue (see page 7).
4. Blow up a balloon until it's firm, but not overly taut, and tie the open end into a knot.

5. Dip a strip of newspaper into the glue, and wipe off any excess with your fingers. Then place the strip onto the balloon.

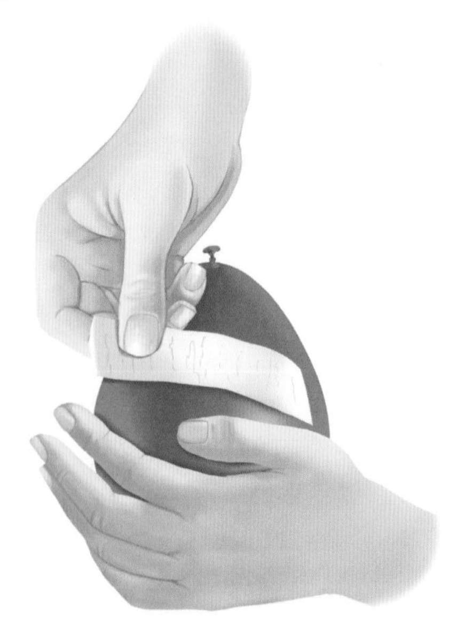

6. Keep repeating this process, laying the strips in neat lines until your balloon is totally covered, except for the small hole where the balloon tie pokes out.

7. Add a second layer of glue-coated newspaper strips in the opposite direction. Try to make them as even as possible. Keep in mind that using any more than two layers of newspaper strips can make your piñata too hard to break open, but this might be perfect if you want to use your piñata for decoration or storage and want to make it stronger.

8. Once you have finished applying the glue and paper, set your model aside for 24 hours. If you do not allow it to completely dry, the glue may become mouldy.

9. Once your papier-mâché has completely dried, pop the balloon, pull it out through the hole and throw it away.

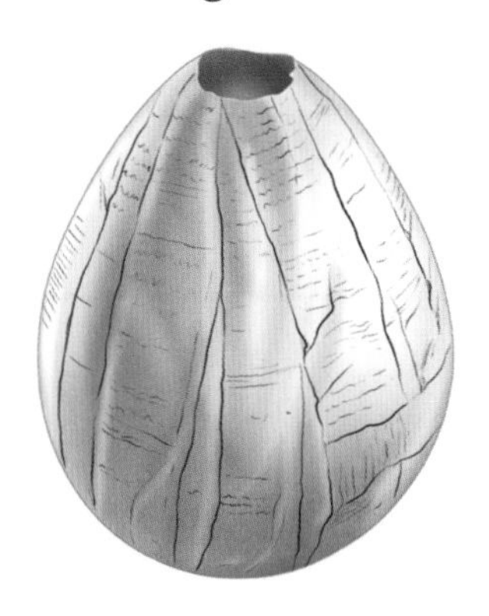

HOW TO MAKE PAPIER-MÂCHÉ GLUE

To make the glue, mix together 1 cup (9.6 fluid oz.) of flour, 1 cup (9.6 fluid oz.) of water and 1 tablespoon (1.2 in US tablespoon size) of salt in a bowl until the mixture is smooth.

Some people have reactions when their skin comes into contact with gluten, which is found in wheat flour. When making papier-mâché glue, you can switch the plain flour to wheat-free cornflour (maize) to avoid this.

Cardboard Mini Piñatas

Constructing mini piñatas from card can be less time-consuming but slightly trickier than making papier-mâché. The benefit is that you can make a piñata in pretty much any shape you can imagine. The card models consist of two identical halves held apart by a 'spacer strip' that ensures there is room in between the two sides to put your goodies in.

The trick to making a good mini piñata from cardboard is to ensure that you choose a card that is flexible enough to work with easily, but sturdy enough to make sure your model holds its shape. The cardboard from an empty cereal box is ideal!

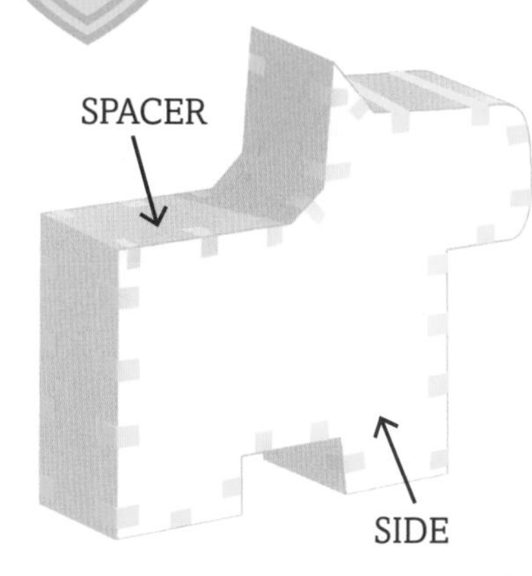

Decorating Your Mini Piñata with Crepe Paper

Piñatas are traditionally covered in fringed crepe paper. You can buy the ready-made fringed paper at craft stores, but it is cheaper to buy rolls of crepe paper (such as party streamers) and cut the fringe yourself. You can also buy sheets of crepe paper and cut them into 2.5-cm (1-in) wide strips.

When applying the crepe paper to your piñata, begin at the bottom and work upwards in neat, straight lines. Glue each layer so that it just overlaps the one below.

Painting Your Mini Piñata

Painting your mini piñata instead of covering it with crepe paper can help you to achieve a wide range of styles, colours and effects. If you are going to paint your piñata, make an extra special effort to get a nice, smooth finish on your papier-mâché so that lumps and bumps don't show up on the finished piñata.

It is best to use water-based poster paints that give a nice solid coverage for these projects. For particularly light-coloured paints, you may need to paint a white base coat first and let it dry so that the newspaper does not show through.

Filling Your Mini Piñata

No matter what you choose to put inside your piñata, make sure you only fill it with as much weight as it can hold without sagging, breaking or falling apart. A good rule is to fill it no more than one-quarter full.

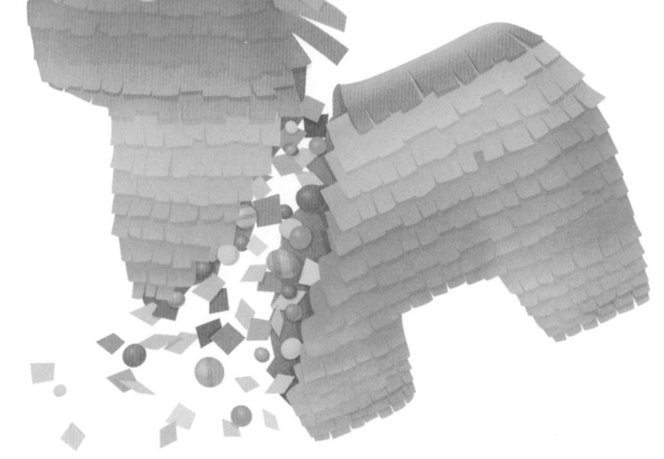

Hanging Your Mini Piñata

In case you want to hang up your finished project, most mini piñatas in this book have four holes around the opening at the top that you can tie your string through. It is important that your holes are not too close to the opening or the string will rip through your piñata and it will fall to the ground when you hang it.

Make the four evenly spaced holes in your piñata by carefully pushing a metal skewer through the papier-mâché, around 2 cm (1 in) below the opening.

If you don't want to hang your piñata, you can skip putting holes in the papier-mâché or cardboard shape.

To thread your string:

1. Push the string in through one hole and out the opposite hole. Keep pulling until you have the same amount of string on both sides.
2. Bring the two ends of the string together in the middle and tie them in a knot.
3. Push each end of the string out one of the remaining side holes.
4. Bring the two pieces of the string together and tie them in a knot in the middle above the opening.
5. You will now be able to use the two loose ends of the string to hang the mini piñata wherever you choose.

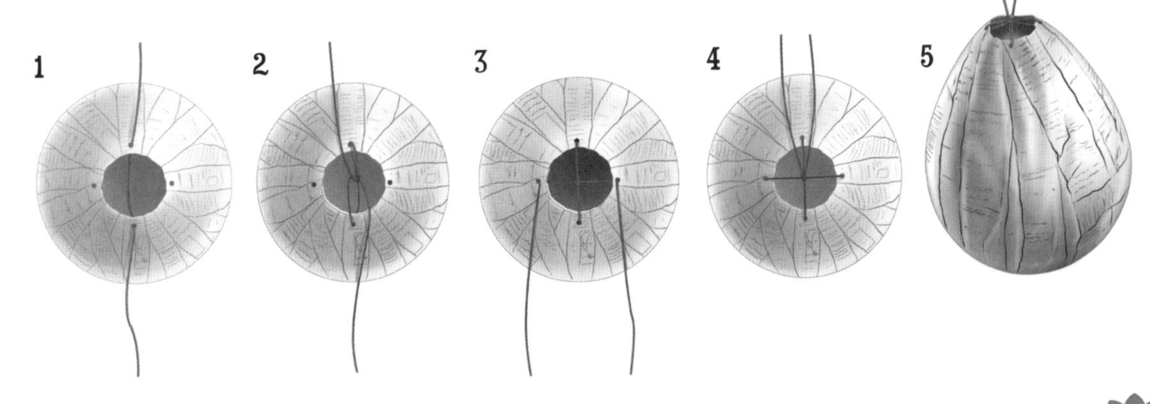

Majestic Lion

This lion, with its magnificent streaming crepe-paper mane, might be small but its effect is huge!

You will need:

- A small balloon
- Two sheets of newspaper, cut into strips
- Papier-mâché glue
- A metal skewer
- A thick paintbrush
- Orange, white and black paint
- A thin paintbrush
- Scissors
- An A5 sheet of orange cardboard
- Craft glue
- Orange, black and brown crepe paper
- Around 2 m (6.5 ft) of thick string or twine

1. Blow your balloon up until it's about the size of your fist, being careful not to overfill it, and tie it off at the end.

2. Cover the balloon with two layers of papier-mâché, using the newspaper and papier-mâché glue. Leave a small hole around the balloon tie (the hole will need to be big enough for you to insert your goodies).

3. Allow to dry and harden for at least 24 hours, then pop the balloon and remove it from your piñata.

4. Use the metal skewer to poke four evenly spaced holes around the top of your piñata, around 2 cm (1 in) below the opening.

5. Paint the whole piñata orange and allow to dry.

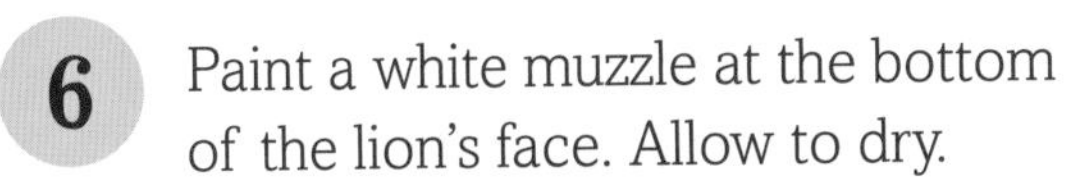

6 Paint a white muzzle at the bottom of the lion's face. Allow to dry.

7 Use a thin paintbrush and black paint for the lion's eyes, nose and mouth.

8 Add black small black dots above the mouth and just under the chin, and whiskers coming out from each side.

9 Cut two round ear shapes from the orange card.

10 Fold a 1-cm (0.5-in) crease along the bottom of each ear. Apply craft glue to the bottom fold and glue the ears to the top sides of the head. Allow to dry.

11 Cut the orange, black and brown crepe paper into lengths of 20 cm (8 in) x 2 cm (1 in). Alternating colours, glue the strips all the way around the edge of the lion's face to make a thick, shaggy mane, as shown on the next page. Allow to dry.

12 If desired, fill the piñata with goodies to around a quarter full.

13 Thread your string through the holes at the top of your piñata (following the instructions on page 9), and your lion is roaring to go!

TRY THIS!

Turn your Majestic Lion into a moneybox! After removing the balloon but before the papier-mâché dries completely, press the bottom of the lion's head to make a flat surface. Cover the hole in the top of the lion's head with more papier-mâché, but leave a coin-sized hole.

Buzzy Bee

This beautiful busy bee is sure to create a buzz – and the best part about him is that he doesn't sting!

You will need:

- A small balloon
- Two sheets of newspaper, cut into strips
- Papier-mâché glue
- Around 2 m (6.5 ft) of thick string or twine
- Masking tape
- A thick paintbrush
- Yellow and black paint
- A pencil (optional)
- A metal skewer
- Craft glue
- Two black pipe cleaners
- Two googly eyes
- A thin paintbrush
- Scissors
- One A4 sheet of white or off-white tracing paper or almost see-through paper
- An A5 sheet of black card

1. Blow your balloon up until it's about the size of your fist, being careful not to overfill it, and tie it off at the end.

2. Cover the balloon with two layers of papier-mâché, using the newspaper and papier-mâché glue. Leave a small hole around the balloon tie (the hole will need to be big enough for you to insert your goodies).

3. Allow to dry and harden for at least 24 hours, then pop the balloon and remove it from your piñata.

4. The opening will be at the back of your piñata. If you are going to hang your bee, you can loop your string twice around the middle of your piñata and tie it firmly at the top. Separate the two loops so that they support the bee's weight evenly and secure the string in place with masking tape.

5. Paint the whole piñata yellow, ensuring you cover the string and masking tape. Allow to dry.

6. Paint three black stripes around the middle of your piñata and allow to dry. You can sketch your lines out in pencil first to help keep them nice and tidy if you like.

7. Use the skewer to poke two holes in the top of the head where the antennae will go.

8. Put some glue on the end of each pipe cleaner and push them through the holes you made on top. Apply some extra glue to the tops of the holes where the pipe cleaners come out so that they stay firmly in place. Allow to dry.

9. Curl the end of each pipe cleaner into a little spiral.

10. Glue two googly eyes to the bee's face and paint a black smiling mouth underneath, using a thin paintbrush. Allow to dry.

11. Cut out two wing shapes from the tracing paper. Each wing should be around half the length of your piñata.

12. Fold a 1-cm (0.5-in) crease along the bottom of each wing. Apply glue to the bottom fold and stick the wings side by side to the top of the bee's body. Allow to dry.

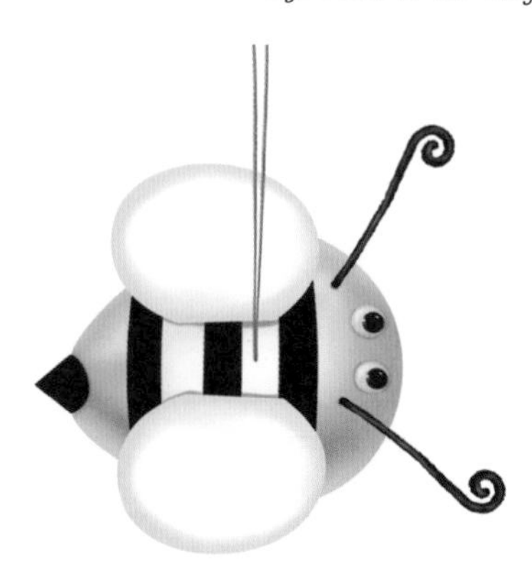

13 If desired, fill the piñata with goodies to around a quarter full. You could even fill it with potpourri (dried flowers) if you wanted to make your room smell nice!

14 Cut a square of black card roughly 5 cm (2 in) along each side. Roll the card into a neat cone shape and fasten the edges together with glue. Once dry, trim the bottom of the cone to make it even. This will be your bee's stinger.

15 Glue the stinger over the opening at the back of the bee. Once it dries, your bee is ready to get busy, storing all sorts of sweet treats!

TRY THIS!

Make lots of mini-piñata bees and a hive for them to live in. To make the hive, blow up a large balloon, papier-mâché it, cut a large hole halfway up the balloon (so no bees will fall out when it's upright) and cover the whole thing in light-brown or yellow paint or crepe paper!

Bouncing Bunny

This adorable little bunny is so appealing, you might want to create a whole burrow full!

You will need:

- A small balloon
- Two sheets of newspaper, cut into strips
- Papier-mâché glue
- A metal skewer
- A thick paintbrush
- White, pink and black paint
- Craft glue
- Two googly eyes
- A thin paintbrush
- Scissors
- An A4 sheet of white cardboard
- An A5 sheet of black cardboard
- Around 2 m (6.5 ft) of thick string or twine

1. Blow your balloon up until it's about the size of your fist, being careful not to overfill it, and tie it off at the end.

2. Cover the balloon with two layers of papier-mâché, using the newspaper and papier-mâché glue. Leave a small hole around the balloon tie (the hole will need to be big enough for you to insert your goodies).

3. Allow to dry and harden for at least 24 hours, then pop the balloon and remove it from your piñata.

4. Use the metal skewer to poke four evenly spaced holes around the top of your piñata, around 2 cm (1 in) below the opening.

5. Paint the whole piñata white. Allow to dry.

6. Glue two googly eyes to the bunny's face.

7. Use a thin paintbrush to paint a pink triangular nose, with rounded corners, below the eyes.

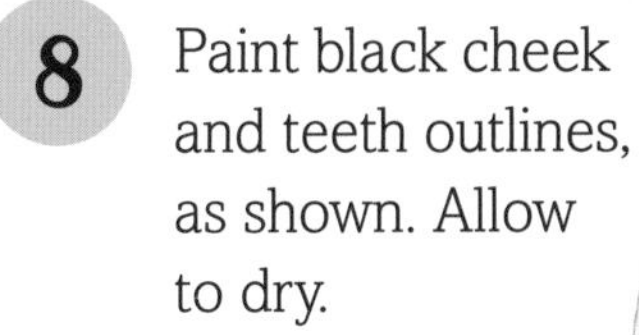

8 Paint black cheek and teeth outlines, as shown. Allow to dry.

9 Cut four rabbit feet and two ears from the white card, in the shapes as shown.

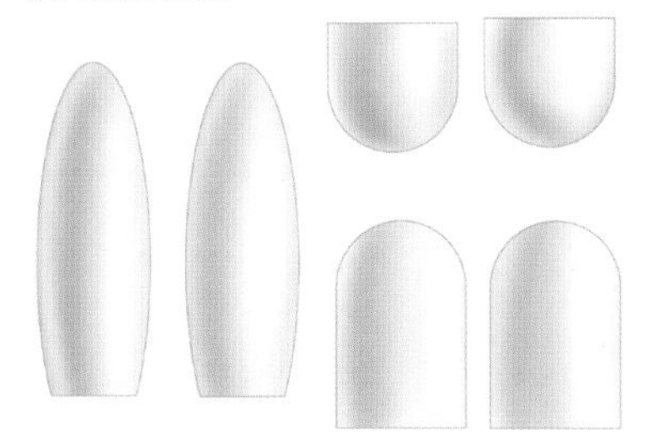

10 Paint the centre of each ear pink, leaving a 1-cm (0.5-in) white border around the edges.

11 When dry, fold a 1-cm (0.5-in) crease along the bottom of each ear. Apply glue to the bottom flaps and glue the ears to the top of the head, just below the opening. Fold the tip of one ear forwards slightly. Allow to dry.

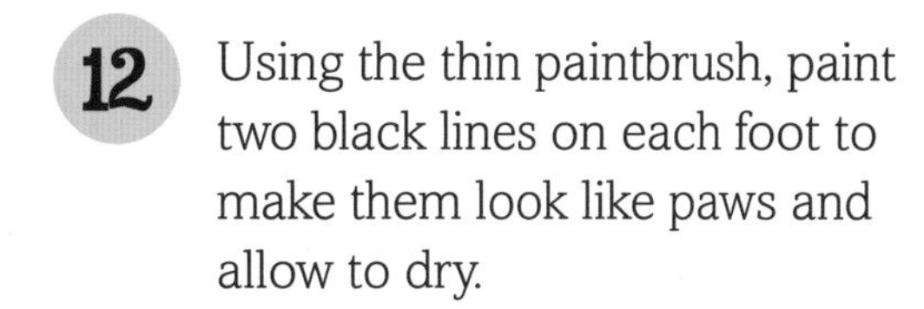

12 Using the thin paintbrush, paint two black lines on each foot to make them look like paws and allow to dry.

13 Glue two feet to the bottom of the bunny, so that its toes stick out, and two feet to the front, about one-quarter of the way from the bottom.

TRY THIS!

You can paint your bunny any colour you like! Why not try a pink bunny with white ears, or even a super-bright blue or green bunny?

14 Cut six thin strips of black card to make whiskers. Glue three whiskers to each of the bunny's cheeks. Allow to dry.

15 If desired, fill the piñata with goodies to around a quarter full.

16 Thread your string through the holes at the top of your piñata (following the instructions on page 9) and it's ready to bounce! Attaching its string to a stick will help it hop along.

TRY THIS!

Turn this mini piñata into the perfect holiday gift by filling it with small chocolate eggs with a note to give it to your best buddy!

Jack-o'-lantern

People have been carving scary jack-o'-lanterns for hundreds of years, but a jack-o'-lantern piñata is sweet as well as spooky!

You will need:

- A small, round balloon
- Two sheets of newspaper, cut into strips
- Papier-mâché glue
- A metal skewer
- Scissors
- Strips of orange crepe paper, enough to cover the whole balloon
- Craft glue
- An A4 sheet of black cardboard
- Around 2 m (6.5 ft) of thick string or twine

1. Blow your balloon up until it's about the size of your fist, being careful not to overfill it, and tie it off at the end.

2. Cover the balloon with two layers of papier-mâché, using the newspaper and papier-mâché glue. Leave a small hole around the balloon tie (the hole will need to be big enough for you to insert your goodies).

3. Allow to dry and harden for at least 24 hours, then pop the balloon and remove it from your piñata.

4. Use the metal skewer to poke four evenly spaced holes around the top of your piñata, around 2 cm (1 in) below the opening.

5. Cut slits all the way along your strips of crepe paper, spacing each slit around 1 cm (0.5 in) apart to create a fringed effect.

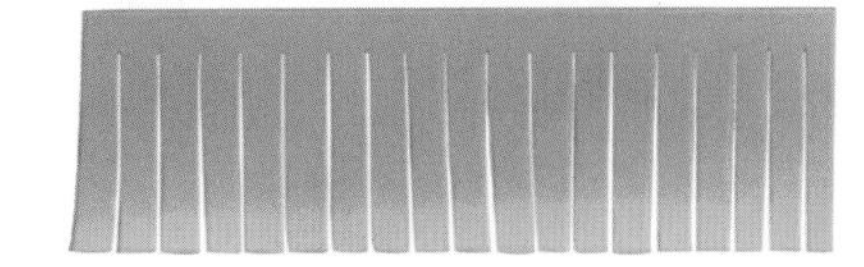

6 Use craft glue to stick the strips of crepe paper onto the piñata in neat layers, covering the entire surface so that none of the newspaper shows through. Allow to dry.

7 Cut two large triangular eyes and a small triangular nose from the black card.

8 Cut a jagged mouth shape and a pumpkin stalk from the black card, as shown.

9 Glue the eyes, nose and mouth to the front of the piñata.

10 Glue the stalk to the top. Allow to dry.

11 If desired, fill the piñata with goodies to around a quarter full.

12 Thread your string through the holes at the top of your piñata (following the instructions on page 9) and it's ready to go!

TRY THIS!

To decorate your house or bedroom during Halloween, make at least five mini jack-o'-lanterns and string them together to make a garland. Try giving them all different spooky faces!

Friendly Penguin

Penguins live in some of the world's coldest places, but this adorable little one can hang out anywhere you choose!

You will need:

- A small balloon
- Two sheets of newspaper, cut into strips
- Papier-mâché glue
- A metal skewer
- A paintbrush
- White and black paint
- Scissors
- An A5 sheet of black cardboard
- Craft glue
- Two googly eyes
- An A5 sheet of orange cardboard
- Around 2 m (6.5 ft) of thick string or twine

1. Blow your balloon up until it's about the size of your fist, being careful not to overfill it, and tie it off at the end.

2. Cover the balloon with two layers of papier-mâché, using the newspaper and papier-mâché glue. Leave a small hole around the balloon tie (the hole will need to be big enough for you to insert your goodies).

3. Allow to dry and harden for at least 24 hours, then pop the balloon and remove it from your piñata.

4. Use the metal skewer to poke four evenly spaced holes around the top of the piñata, around 2 cm (1 in) below the opening.

5. Paint the penguin's stomach and face area white. The top of the face should be a love heart shape, as shown.

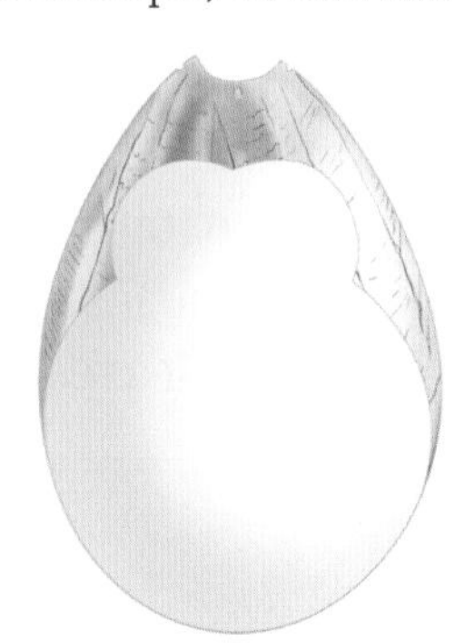

6 Paint the rest of the piñata black. Allow to dry.

7 Cut two flipper shapes from the black card and glue them to the sides of the penguin's body.

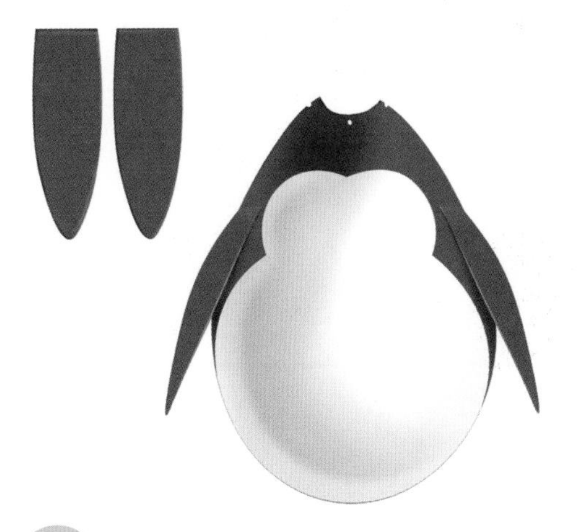

8 Glue two googly eyes to the face.

9 Cut two feet from the orange card and glue them to the bottom of the piñata so that they poke out from under the penguin's body.

10 Cut a diamond shape from the orange card. Fold it in half to make a beak shape. Glue the folded edge of the beak below the eyes.

11 Cut a bow tie shape from the black card. Glue the bow tie under the beak. Allow all of the glue to dry.

12 If desired, fill the piñata with goodies to around a quarter full.

13 Thread your string through the holes at the top of your piñata (following the instructions on page 9) and it's ready to waddle!

TRY THIS!

Turn your piñata into a pen holder by enlarging the opening at the top so that you can stand pens and pencils in it. You may also need to make the feet out of extra-thick card to help the penguin stand upright on your desk. Filling your penguin up with some rice will also help to keep it standing straight on the table.

Magical Unicorn

For this project, you'll be transforming a humble mini-piñata donkey into a mystical unicorn!

You will need:

- Two A4 sheets of white cardboard
- An A4 sheet of tracing paper or access to a photocopier
- A graphite pencil
- Scissors
- Masking tape
- Around 2 m (6.5 ft) of thick string or twine
- Strips of white crepe paper, enough to cover your whole unicorn
- Craft glue
- Two googly eyes
- An A5 sheet of blue card
- Around 1.2 m (4 ft) in total of paper strips or curling ribbon, in a range of bright colours

1 Fold one piece of white card in half along the short edge.

2 Use tracing paper to trace the unicorn template on page 46, or photocopy the template. Cut out the traced or photocopied shape and place it on top of your folded card. Use the pencil to trace the unicorn shape onto the card.

3 Keeping the card folded, cut out the shape. You should now have two matching sides of a unicorn. You can ask an adult for help with this step.

4 Cut three 2.5-cm (1-in) wide strips lengthways from the second sheet of card. These strips will be used to make a spacer between the two halves of your unicorn.

5 Use masking tape to attach one of the strips to the edge of one of the unicorn halves so that it sticks out sideways (at a 90-degree angle) and follows the shape of the unicorn, as shown in step 6, below. The strip of card will sit in between the two sides of the unicorn's body. Add a second strip, and a third one if needed, until you have gone all the way around the unicorn shape. Be careful not to add too much masking tape (it's best if you leave some gaps in between) so that it breaks apart easily enough if you decide to use it as a piñata to smash. Otherwise, make it more secure by adding more tape.

6 Use masking tape to stick the second unicorn half to the other edge of the card strips. You should now have a completely enclosed unicorn shape.

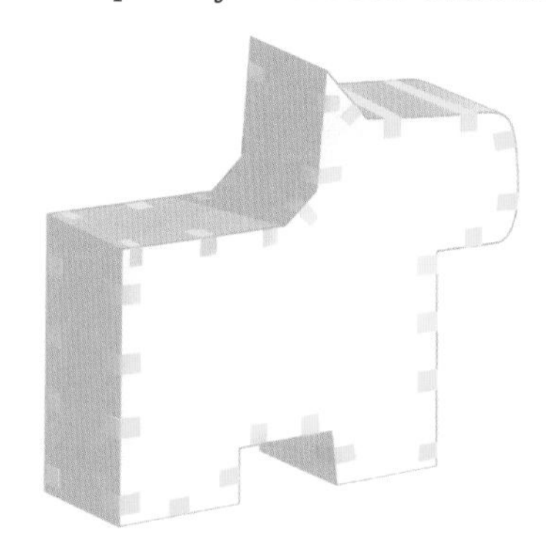

7 Cut a hole at the rear of the unicorn where the tail will go. Ensure it is big enough to fit goodies inside, if you want to add them.

8 Tie your string in a double loop around the unicorn's belly, leaving one end of the string long enough to hang your piñata. Pull the two loops apart and secure the string to the body with masking tape.

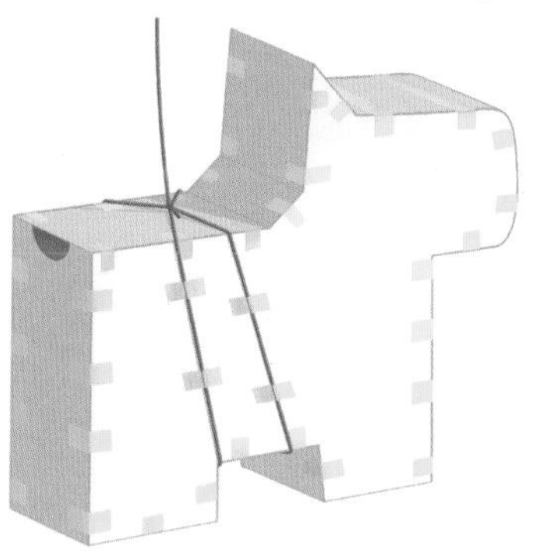

9 Cut slits all the way along your strips of crepe paper, spacing each slit around 1 cm (0.5 in) apart to create a fringed effect.

10 Use craft glue to stick the strips of crepe paper onto the piñata in neat layers, covering the entire surface so that none of the card or the string (apart from the length left for hanging) shows through. Allow to dry.

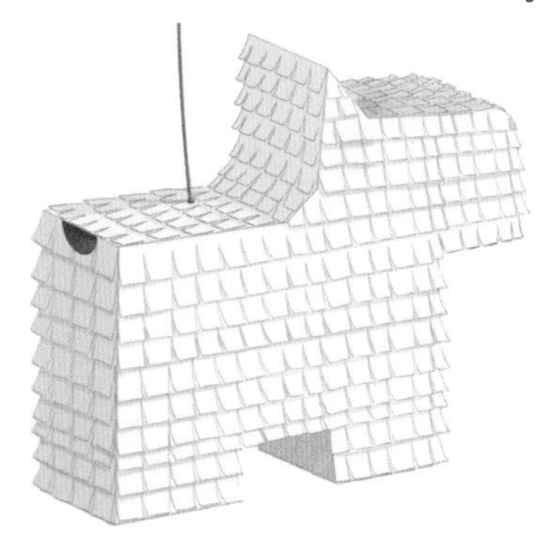

11 Stick a googly eye to each side of the unicorn's face and allow to dry.

TRY THIS!

Use these mini piñatas as funky table decorations for your next party. You can also fill them with confetti or glitter to make party poppers. You can even fill them with sweets and give them to your guests in place of goody bags!

12 Cut a square of blue card roughly 5 cm (2 in) along each side. Roll the card into a neat cone shape and fasten the edges together with glue. This will be your unicorn's horn.

13 Once the glue has dried, trim the bottom of the horn so that it is even and glue it to the top of the unicorn's head.

14 Cut the pieces of paper or curling ribbon into 10-cm (4-in) lengths. Secure them in a bunch by folding them together and wrapping masking tape tightly around one end. This will be your unicorn's tail.

15 Ask for an adult's help to curl the ends of the paper around a pencil or to curl the ribbon by running one scissor blade down the ribbed side. Start curling some strands about three-quarters of the way up and others further down so that they fall in a nice cascade rather than all bunching up in the same place.

Scissors can be sharp! Be super careful not to cut yourself when curling your ribbon.

16 If desired, fill the piñata with goodies to around a quarter full.

17 Insert the gathered end of the tail into the opening at the back of your unicorn and secure in place with masking tape. If it looks untidy, cover the area with extra crepe paper. Now your little unicorn is ready to create magic!

Today's hot-air balloons are powered by heated gas, but this cute mini piñata is powered by your imagination!

You will need:

- A small round balloon
- Two sheets of newspaper, cut into strips
- Papier-mâché glue
- Scissors
- Scalloping scissors (optional)
- Strips of green crepe paper, enough to cover the whole balloon
- Craft glue
- Around 1.5 m (5 ft) of pink ribbon
- An A5 sheet of pale-pink paper
- An A5 sheet of pale-yellow paper
- A paintbrush
- Pink paint
- A small cardboard cup or egg carton cup, or a box roughly 5 cm (2 in) wide
- A metal skewer
- Masking tape
- Around 2.5 m (8 ft) of thick string or twine

1. Blow your balloon up until it's about the size of your fist, being careful not to overfill it, and tie it off at the end. The end with the tie will become the bottom of your hot-air balloon.

2. Cover the balloon with two layers of papier-mâché, using the newspaper and papier-mâché glue. Leave a small hole around the balloon tie (the hole will need to be big enough for you to insert your goodies).

3. Allow to dry and harden for at least 24 hours, then pop the balloon and remove it from your piñata.

4. Cut a wavy pattern all along the bottom edge of your strips of crepe paper to create a scalloped effect or use scalloping scissors (available from most craft stores, which will make this a lot quicker). Stack several strips of paper together so that you can cut multiple pieces at once.

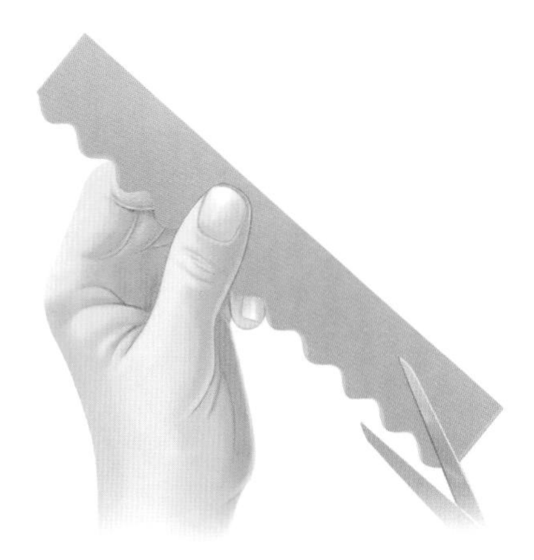

5. Use craft glue to stick the strips of crepe paper onto the piñata in neat layers, covering the entire surface so that none of the newspaper shows through. Allow to dry.

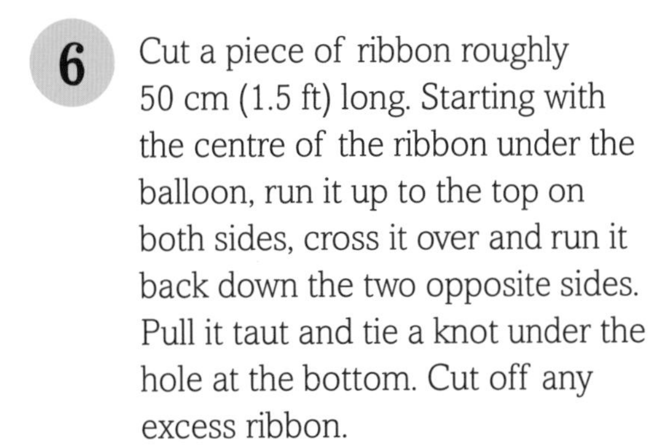

6. Cut a piece of ribbon roughly 50 cm (1.5 ft) long. Starting with the centre of the ribbon under the balloon, run it up to the top on both sides, cross it over and run it back down the two opposite sides. Pull it taut and tie a knot under the hole at the bottom. Cut off any excess ribbon.

7. Cut a length of ribbon long enough to go around the widest part of your balloon one and a half times.

8. Cut twenty triangles, around 1.5 cm (0.5 in) high, ten from the pink paper and ten from the yellow paper.

9. Fold the bottom of each triangle over the edge of the ribbon, alternating between evenly spaced pink and yellow triangles, and glue it in place, to make bunting. Allow to dry.

10. Drape the bunting around your balloon about one-third of the way down from the top then loop it around one-third of the way up from the bottom and glue in place.

11. Paint your paper cup or box pink. Allow to dry.

12. Use the metal skewer to poke four evenly spaced holes around 2 cm (1 in) below the rim of the cup or box.

13. Cut four pieces of ribbon around 10 cm (4 in) long.

14. Push the end of one piece of ribbon through one of the holes in the cup or box and tie a knot in the end so that it can't slip back out. Tie the other end to one of the pieces of ribbon wrapped around the balloon, close to the bottom.

15. Repeat with the remaining three pieces of ribbon, tying one between each hole in the cup or box and each side of the balloon.

16. If desired, fill the piñata with goodies to around a quarter full.

17. Use masking tape to patch up the hole securely and cover with extra crepe paper to make it neat. Turn the balloon right way up.

18. Thread the string underneath the ribbon that crosses over at the top of the balloon and your piñata is ready to soar!

TRY THIS!

Turn your hot-air balloon into a hanging storage feature for your bedroom. Instead of filling the balloon with goodies, simply hang the piñata in the corner of your room and fill the basket with anything you like – or even try a lightweight mini pot plant, like a succulent!

Crazy Monster

Some monsters are super scary and some are totally bizarre, but this crazy monster is a real scream! It also looks great in green or blue.

You will need:

- A small round balloon
- Two sheets of newspaper, cut into strips
- Papier-mâché glue
- A metal skewer
- Scissors
- Strips of pink crepe paper, enough to cover the whole balloon
- Craft glue
- An A5 sheet of white cardboard
- An A5 sheet of black cardboard
- Around 2 m (6.5 ft) of thick string or twine

1. Blow your balloon up until it's about the size of your fist, being careful not to overfill it, and tie it off at the end.

2. Cover the balloon with two layers of papier-mâché, using the newspaper and papier-mâché glue. Leave a small hole around the balloon tie (the hole will need to be big enough for you to insert your goodies).

3. Allow to dry and harden for at least 24 hours, then pop the balloon and remove it from your piñata.

4. Use the metal skewer to poke four evenly spaced holes around the top of the piñata, around 2 cm (1 in) below the opening.

5. Cut slits all the way along your strips of crepe paper, spacing each slit around 1 cm (0.5 in) apart to create a fringed effect.

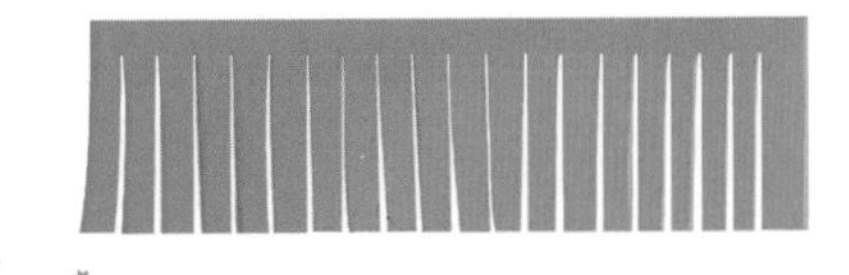

6 Use craft glue to stick the strips of crepe paper onto the piñata in neat layers, covering the entire surface so that none of the newspaper shows through. Allow to dry.

7 Cut a circle around 2 cm (1 in) wide from white card for the monster's single eye.

8 Cut a circle about half the size of the eye from black card for the pupil. Glue the black circle onto the white circle.

9 Glue the eye onto the upper front part of the monster's face.

10 Cut two foot shapes from the white card. Cut out footpad shapes for each foot from black card, as shown. Glue the footpad shapes to the feet.

11 Glue the feet to the lower front of the monster's body.

12 Cut a moon-shaped mouth from the black card. Cut a square from the white card and glue it to the top right of the black mouth so that it resembles a baby's tooth.

13 Glue the mouth halfway between the eye and the feet.

14 Cut two curved horn shapes from the black card.

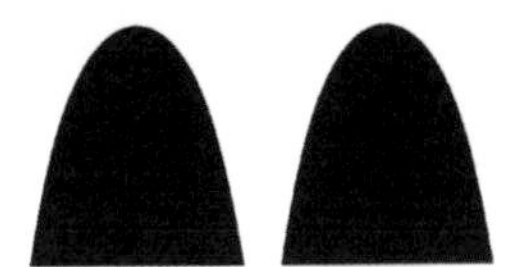

15 Fold a crease along the bottom 1 cm (0.5 in) of each horn. Apply glue to the bottom fold and glue one horn to each side of the top of the head. Allow all of the glue to dry.

16 If desired, fill the piñata with goodies to around a quarter full.

17 Thread your string through the holes at the top of your piñata (following the instructions on page 9) and it's ready to scare!

TRY THIS!

Make a cool lamp by making your mini monster piñata upside down so that the opening sits at the bottom. Instead of attaching the cardboard eye, cut out a hole in the piñata in the shape of an eye. Place the piñata over a small LED light and your little critter will light up in the dark!

Make sure if you are using your piñatas as lampshades, that they are not too close to the light bulb. Also never leave your lamp unattended.

Pretty Pineapple

This mini-piñata pineapple is challenging to create, but the end result is simply gorgeous!

You will need:

- A small balloon
- Two sheets of newspaper, cut into strips
- Papier-mâché glue
- A metal skewer
- Strips of yellow crepe paper, enough to cover your whole piñata one and a half times
- Craft glue
- Scissors
- An A5 sheet of black cardboard
- A small piece of white cardboard
- An A4 sheet of green cardboard
- An A5 sheet of pink cardboard
- Around 2 m (6.5 ft) of thick string or twine

1. Blow your balloon up until it's about the size of your fist, being careful not to overfill it, and tie it off at the end.

2. Cover the balloon with two layers of papier-mâché, using the newspaper and papier-mâché glue. Leave a small hole around the balloon tie (the hole will need to be big enough for you to insert your goodies).

3. Your piñata will take at least 24 hours to dry and harden. If you are not planning to hang up your piñata, then just before it is completely dry, lightly press in the bottom so that it sits flat. Once completely dry, pop the balloon and remove it from your piñata.

4. Use the metal skewer to poke four evenly spaced holes around the top of your piñata, around 2 cm (1 in) below the opening.

5. Cover your whole piñata neatly in strips of yellow crepe paper, gluing them in place. Run the strips diagonally from the bottom left to the top right. Ensure that none of the newspaper shows through. Allow to dry.

6. Glue strips of crepe paper running diagonally in the opposite direction. Leave a 2-cm (1-in) space between each strip so that you end up with a criss-cross finish. Allow to dry.

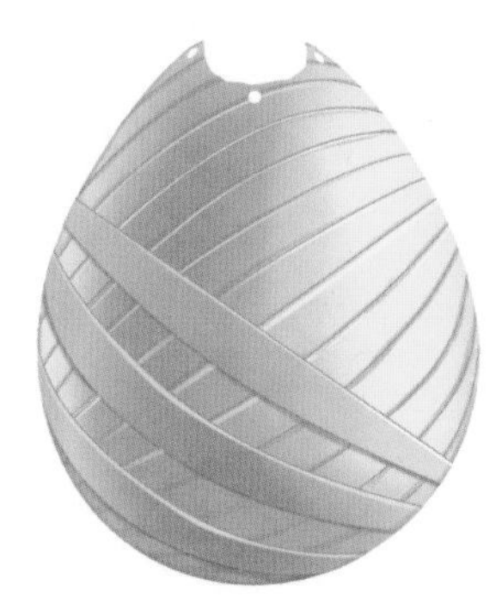

7. Cut three circles around 4 cm (1.5 in) wide from black card. Cut one circle in half to make a mouth shape (you can discard the other half).

8. Cut two tiny circles from white card. Glue these in the top right-hand corners of the two black circles. These are your pineapple's eyes.

9. Glue the mouth to the centre of the pineapple, about three-quarters of the way down. Glue the eyes to the right and left of the mouth, but very slightly above it.

10. Cut four long leaf shapes from green card. Each leaf should be almost as long as the pineapple.

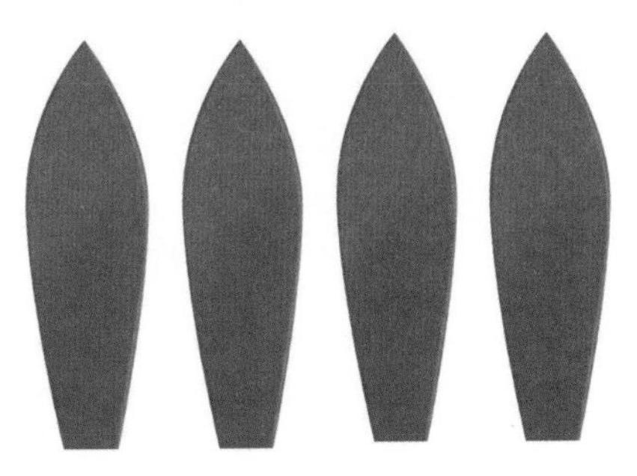

11 Fold a crease along the bottom 1 cm (0.5 in) of each leaf. Apply glue to the bottom flaps and glue the leaves to the very top of the pineapple.

12 Cut a bow shape from the pink card. Glue it just below the leaves, to the top left of the pineapple's face. Allow all of the glue to dry.

13 If desired, fill the piñata with goodies to around a quarter full.

TRY THIS!

To make a funky pineapple earring holder, use a hole punch to make holes along both edges of each leaf, pop an earring into each hole and voila! You have a tropically fresh jewellery holder.

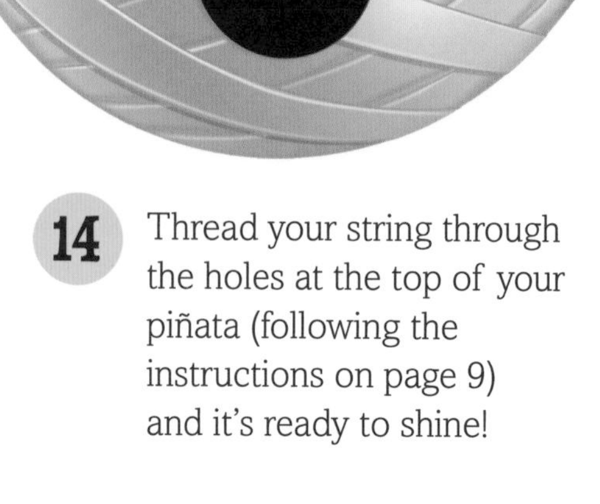

14 Thread your string through the holes at the top of your piñata (following the instructions on page 9) and it's ready to shine!

Fantastic Fish

This vibrant fish is sure to go down swimmingly, whether you use it as an ornament or as a whacking piñata.

You will need:

- A small balloon
- Two sheets of newspaper, cut into strips
- Papier-mâché glue
- Around 2 m (6.5 ft) of thick string or twine
- Masking tape
- A paintbrush
- Purple paint
- Scissors
- An A4 sheet of purple cardboard
- Craft glue
- Large purple sequins, enough to cover the whole balloon
- Two googly eyes

1. Blow your balloon up until it's about the size of your fist, being careful not to overfill it, and tie it off at the end.

2. Cover the balloon with two layers of papier-mâché, using the newspaper and papier-mâché glue. Leave a small hole around the balloon tie (the hole will need to be big enough for you to insert your goodies).

3. Allow to dry and harden for at least 24 hours, then pop the balloon and remove it from your piñata.

4. The opening will be the back of your piñata where the fish's tail will go. Loop your string twice around the middle of your piñata and tie it firmly at the top. Separate the two loops so that they support the fish's weight evenly and secure the string in place with masking tape.

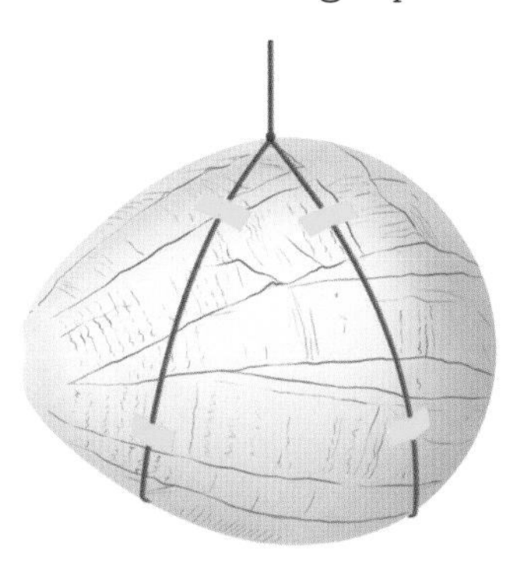

5 Paint the front section of the fish purple. Allow it to dry. This will be the fish's face.

6 Cut two fins, one dorsal fin and one tail from the purple card, in the shapes as shown.

7 Fold a crease along the bottom 1 cm (0.5 in) of the fins and dorsal fin. Apply glue to the flaps and glue a fin to each side of the fish's body and stick the dorsal fin to the top. Allow to dry.

8 Glue the purple sequins all over the fish's body section. Ensure that the sequins are in neat rows and that none of the string (apart from the length at the top that will be used for hanging) or the newspaper shows through. Allow it to dry.

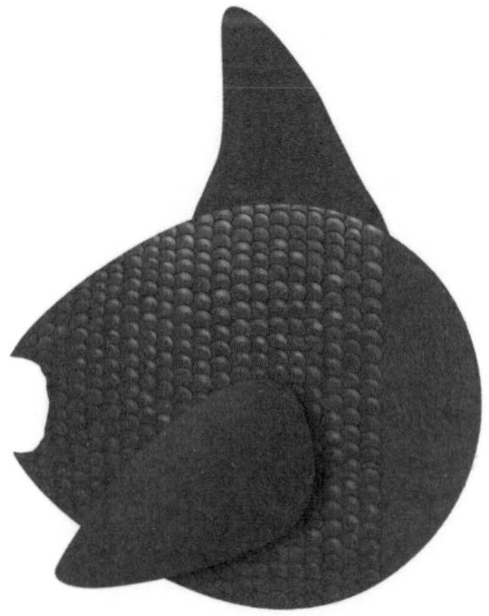

9 Glue a googly eye to each side of the fish's head, in the painted purple section, and allow to dry.

10 If desired, fill the piñata with goodies to around a quarter full. Your fish would also be perfect for storing collected seashells, pretty stones and other natural treasures!

11. Close up the hole at the back with masking tape.

12. Fold a crease along the bottom 1 cm (0.5 in) of the tail. Apply glue to the flap and glue the tail to the back of the fish. Allow it to dry.

13. Add extra sequins around the tail to cover the masking tape and your piñata is ready to swim!

TRY THIS!

Instead of filling it with goodies, create a pet fish by hanging your piñata in a small glass bowl (it can be your new fishbowl!). To do this, tie your fish to a wooden stick that is slightly longer than your fishbowl is wide, and place the stick across the top of the bowl. Make sure that the string is the right length so that your fish hangs in the middle of the bowl, and there you have it – a no-mess, no-fuss fishy friend!

Roaring Rocket

Close your visors, start your engines and get ready for lift-off. But before you shoot for the stars, you'll need to make this mini-piñata rocket!

You will need:

- A small balloon
- Two sheets of newspaper, cut into strips
- Papier-mâché glue
- A metal skewer
- Scissors
- Strips of blue crepe paper, enough to cover the whole balloon
- Two strips of orange crepe paper, around 6 cm (2 in) each
- Craft glue
- An A5 sheet of orange cardboard
- An A4 sheet of green cardboard
- Around 2 m (6.5 ft) of thick string or twine

1. Blow your balloon up until it's about the size of your fist, being careful not to overfill it, and tie it off at the end.

2. Cover the balloon with two layers of papier-mâché, using the newspaper and papier-mâché glue. Leave a small hole around the balloon tie (the hole will need to be big enough for you to insert your goodies).

3. Allow to dry and harden for at least 24 hours, then pop the balloon and remove it from your piñata.

4. Use the metal skewer to poke four evenly spaced holes around the piñata, around 2 cm (1 in) below the opening.

5. Cut slits all the way along the blue and orange strips of crepe paper, spacing each slit around 1 cm (0.5 in) apart to create a fringed effect.

6 Use craft glue to stick the strips of blue crepe paper onto the piñata in neat layers, covering the entire surface so that none of the newspaper shows through. Allow to dry.

7 Cut a strip of orange card around 6 cm (2 in) long and 2.5 cm (1 in) wide.

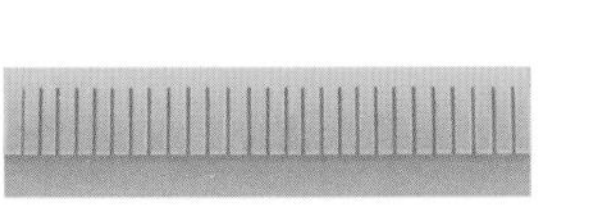

8 Cover the orange card with two layers of fringed orange crepe paper. Curl the strip into a ring and glue the ends together.

9 Glue the orange ring to the bottom of the rocket (the end opposite the opening), as shown. Allow it to dry. This will be the lift-off fire from the rocket's booster!

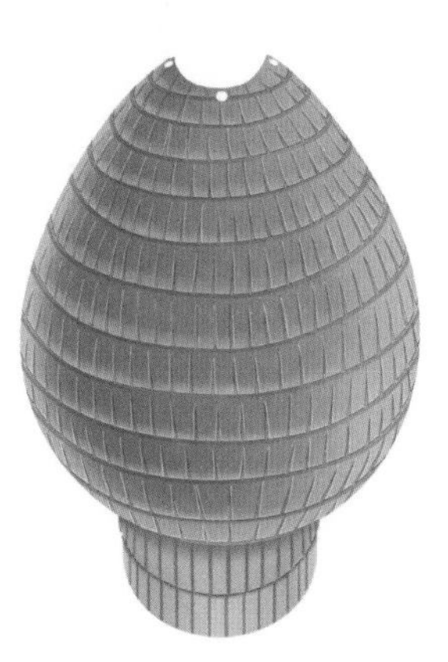

10 Cut three rocket legs from green card, as shown. Each leg should be just under half of the length of the rocket's body.

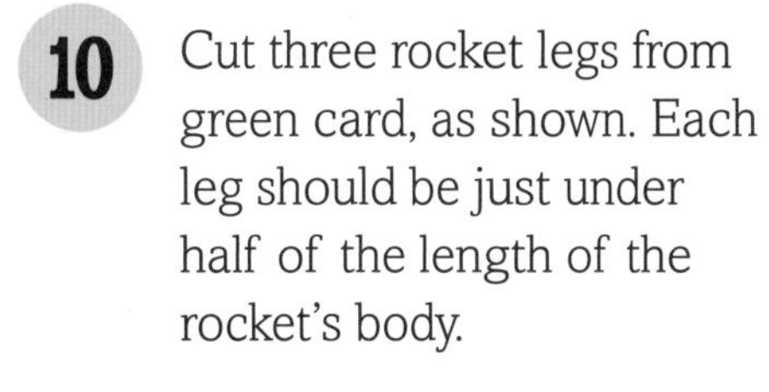

11 Fold a crease along the inside 1 cm (0.5 in) of each leg. Apply glue to the folds and glue the three legs evenly around the base of the rocket, around two-thirds of the way down from the top. Note that these legs will not hold the weight of your piñata, so continue to work with it on its side. Allow it to dry.

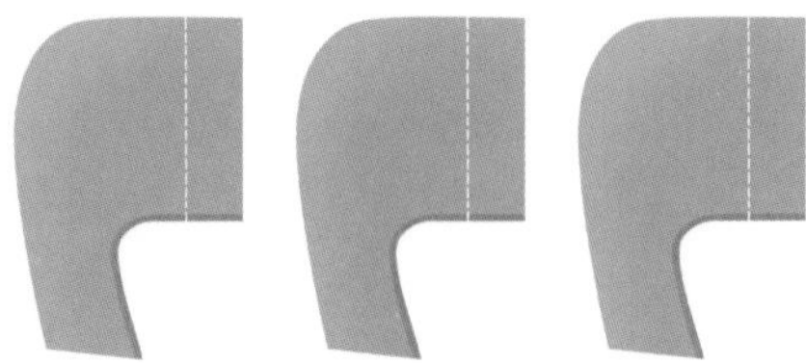

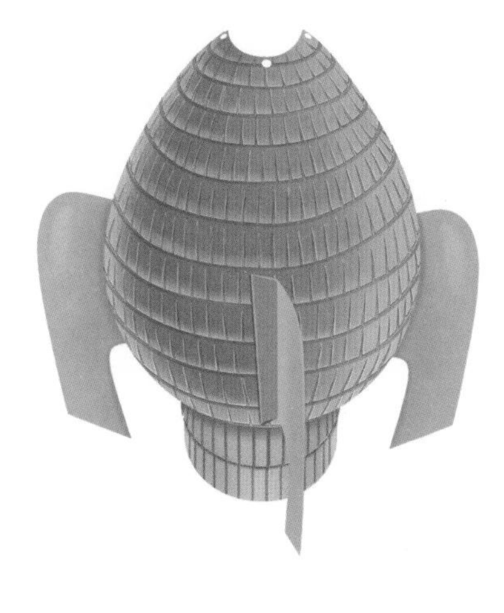

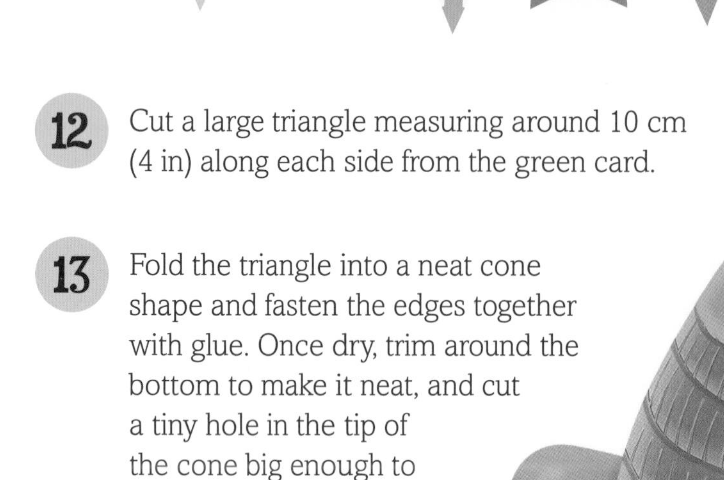

12 Cut a large triangle measuring around 10 cm (4 in) along each side from the green card.

13 Fold the triangle into a neat cone shape and fasten the edges together with glue. Once dry, trim around the bottom to make it neat, and cut a tiny hole in the tip of the cone big enough to fit the string through.

14 If desired, fill the piñata with goodies to around a quarter full.

15 Thread your string through the holes at the top of your piñata (following the instructions on page 9).

16 Thread the end of the string through the hole in the tip of the cone.

17 Slide the cone down over the piñata to form the rocket's nose and glue the bottom of the cone in place. Your rocket mini piñata is now ready to blast off!

TRY THIS!

Make a mini rocket piñata and several round piñatas, painted to look like planets. String them together to make an awesome space mobile that is out of this world!

Fabulous Flamingo

Flamingos are born grey, but the shrimp and algae they eat turns them pink! Create your own fabulous pink flamingo with this project – no shrimp or algae required!

You will need:

- Scissors
- An A4 sheet of white cardboard
- An A4 sheet of tracing paper or access to a photocopier
- A graphite pencil
- Masking tape
- Two pink pipe cleaners
- Around 2 m (6.5 ft) of thick string or twine
- Strips of pink crepe paper, enough to cover your whole flamingo
- Craft glue
- Strip of black crepe paper, 5 cm (2 in) long

1 Cut two strips lengthways down the edges of the white card, around 2.5 cm (1 in) wide.

2 Fold the remaining white card in half along the short side.

3 Use tracing paper to trace the flamingo template on page 47, or photocopy the template. Cut out the shape from the tracing paper or photocopied paper and place it on top of your folded card. Use your pencil to trace the flamingo shape onto your card. Keeping the card folded, cut out the shape. Ask an adult for help with this step if you need to. You should now have two matching sides of a flamingo.

4 Use masking tape to attach one of the strips to the edge of one of the flamingo halves so that it sticks out sideways (at a 90-degree angle) and follows the shape of the flamingo, as shown in step 6. The strip of card will sit in between the two sides of the flamingo's body. Add the second strip and keep going until you have gone all the way around the flamingo shape. Be careful not to add too much masking tape (it's best if you leave some gaps in between) so that it breaks apart easily if you decide to use it as a piñata to smash. Otherwise you can secure it with more tape.

5 Use masking tape to stick the second flamingo half to the other edge of the card strips, but leave one section open so that you can fill the piñata around a quarter full with goodies.

6 Seal up the open section with masking tape. You should now have a completely enclosed flamingo shape.

7 Pass your string under the centre card strip at the top middle of the flamingo's back. Wrap the string around twice and secure in place with masking tape.

8 Stick the two pink pipe cleaners to the bottom of the flamingo's body with masking tape to make legs. Bend one pipe cleaner at knee height so that it looks like your flamingo is standing on one leg. Bend the bottom 1 cm (0.5 in) of each pipe cleaner out to make feet.

9 Cut slits all the way along your strips of pink crepe paper, spacing each slit around 1 cm (0.5 in) apart to create a fringed effect.

10 Use craft glue to stick the strips of crepe paper onto the flamingo's body in neat layers, covering the entire surface, except for the beak, so that none of the card shows through. Allow to dry.

11 Cut two small circles from the black crepe paper. Glue one on each side of the flamingo's face, just behind and a little higher than the beak.

12 Cover the beak with the remaining black crepe paper, and your flamingo mini piñata is ready to fly!

TRY THIS!

Create a striking piece of wall art by painting a blue lake on a canvas, then gluing two flamingo mini piñatas onto it. Have the flamingos facing each other and arrange the pipe-cleaner legs so they look like they are doing a funky flamingo dance!

Mini-piñata Templates

Use these templates to create the Magical Unicorn on page 25 and the Fabulous Flamingo on page 43.

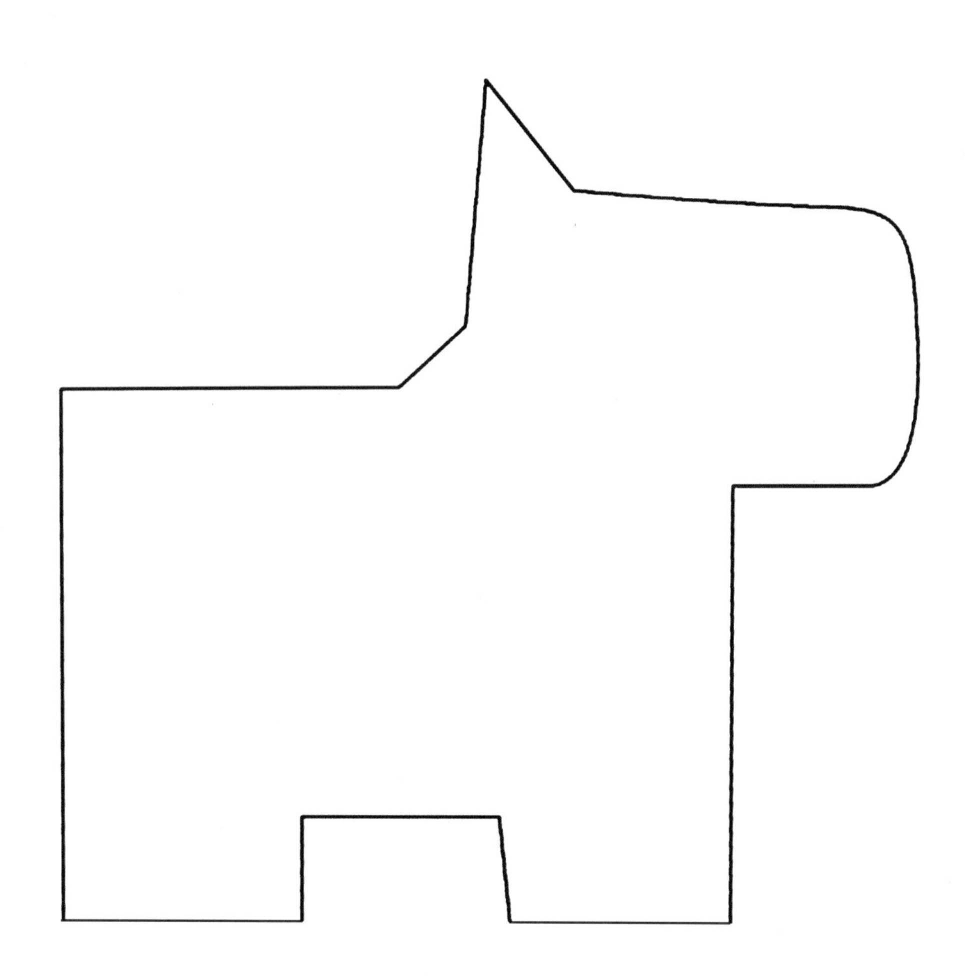

Make a Mini-piñata Whacking Stick!

You can use any old wooden item, such as a wooden spoon handle or rolling pin, or a piece of wooden dowel as a whacking stick, but why not make a cool whacking stick that colour-coordinates with your mini piñata? It's as simple as this:

1. Find a wooden dowel (a rounded stick) 20–30 cm (8–12 in) long from any hardware or timber-supply store.

2. Choose strips of crepe paper that match your piñata; use multiple colours if you like! Cut narrow slits all along the crepe paper to make a fringe.

3. Glue the crepe paper in a spiral from the bottom of the stick almost all the way to the top, leaving around 10 cm (4 in) bare as a handle. Ensure each layer of crepe paper just slightly covers the previous one so the wood doesn't show through. Allow to dry. Alternatively, wrap the stick with different-coloured ribbons.

And there you have it – a fabulous whacking stick that's ready to go!

Once your whacking stick has done its job, simply strip the paper off and put it away, ready to decorate it again to match your next piñata!